THE CHANGING EARTH

AS THE EARTH TURNS

Lynn M. Stone

The Rourke Book Co., Inc.
Vero Beach, Florida 32964

Edited by Sandra A. Robinson

PHOTO CREDITS
Courtesy NASA: cover, pages 4, 7, 8, 10; © Lynn M. Stone: title
page, pages 12, 13, 15, 17, 18, 21

Library of Congress Cataloging-in-Publication Data

Stone, Lynn M.
    The changing earth / by Lynn M. Stone.
        p. cm. — (As the earth turns)
    Includes index.
    ISBN 1-55916-017-9
    1. Earth—Juvenile literature. 2. Astronomy—Juvenile literature.
[1. Earth. 2. Astronomy.] I. Title. II. Series: Stone, Lynn M.
As the earth turns.
QB631.4.S76   1994
525—dc20   93-41103
                                                        CIP
                                                        AC

TABLE OF CONTENTS

The Ball-Shaped Earth   5

The Orbiting Earth   6

The Spinning Earth   9

Gravity   11

Circling the Sun   14

Days and Nights   16

The Earth's Halves   19

Changing Seasons   20

The Tides   22

Glossary   23

Index   24

THE BALL-SHAPED EARTH

The Earth is round like a kickball, but it isn't soft and air-filled. It's hard, and it's filled with metal and rock.

The Earth is one of nine large, round masses in space called **planets.** The sun, planets and several smaller heavenly bodies make up our **solar system.**

The Earth (lower right) is
part of the solar system

THE ORBITING EARTH

The Earth travels in a circle around the sun once each year. The Earth's path around the sun is its **orbit.**

Each planet has a different orbit around the sun. Six planets are farther from the sun than Earth. Mercury and Venus have closer orbits.

The Earth (left) orbits completely around the sun once each year

THE SPINNING EARTH

While it journeys in orbit, the Earth spins, or rotates. Because of its shape and motion, the Earth acts something like a spinning, tilting top.

Just like a top, the Earth has two ends. They are known as poles. The upper end is the north pole. The lower is the south pole.

The Earth spins on its **axis,** an imaginary tilted line from one pole to the other.

Earth's upper end, the north pole, shows in this view of Earth taken from outer space

GRAVITY

The Earth stays in orbit around the sun because of **gravity.** Gravity is a powerful, invisible pulling force. The sun's gravity keeps the Earth in place in the solar system.

The Earth also has its own gravity. That gravity keeps Earth creatures, like us, from floating off into space. Earth's gravity also keeps the moon in an orbit around Earth.

The force of gravity keeps the Earth in an orbit around the sun (upper right)

Low tide leaves a fisherman's rowboats high and dry until the next high tide

Not all parts of Earth get equal amounts of sunlight,
and polar oceans have ice year-round

CIRCLING THE SUN

The sun is a massive fireball in space. Even though the sun is about 93 million miles away, some of its heat and light reach Earth.

The Earth is always moving through space and changing its tilt toward the sun. Because of this, the amount of heat and light reaching Earth changes, too.

The sun's heat and light make life possible on Earth

DAYS AND NIGHTS

As the Earth spins, some parts of it face the sun, while other parts face away. The part of the Earth facing the sun enjoys daylight. The other part has night.

Each day, every part of the Earth has its turn with both daylight and darkness.

As western North America faces the sun, a new day begins

THE EARTH'S HALVES

Around the Earth's middle is an imaginary line called the **equator.** The equator separates the northern and southern halves of the Earth. Each half is called a **hemisphere.**

The north pole is at the top of the northern hemisphere. The south pole is at the bottom of the southern hemisphere. Canada, Mexico and the United States are among the countries in the northern hemisphere.

It's November in the southern hemisphere, and spring flowers bloom in Australia

CHANGING SEASONS

The exact angle of sunlight striking Earth changes slightly every day. That happens because the tilted Earth is traveling around the sun. As the angle changes, the seasons change.

When the northern half of the Earth is tilted toward the sun, it has longer days, and spring and summer. At the same time, the southern hemisphere has shorter days, and fall and winter.

Long periods of sunlight and rapid plant growth are signs of summer in North America

THE TIDES

Each day the moon orbits around the Earth. The moon's gravity, pulling on the Earth, is the major reason for ocean **tides.** A tide is a daily change in ocean level.

A high tide is when the ocean water is highest on the shore. That happens when the moon's pull is strongest.

Most ocean shores have two high tides and two low tides each day.

Glossary

axis (AX iss) — a straight line on which a body rotates

equator (ee KWAY ter) — the imaginary line drawn on maps around the Earth's middle at an equal distance from the north and south poles

gravity (GRAV ih tee) — a powerful, invisible natural force that holds things in place

hemisphere (HEHM iss fear) — either the northern or southern half of the Earth, using the equator as a divider

orbit (OR bit) — the path that an object follows as it repeatedly travels around another object in space

planet (PLAN it) — any one of the nine large, ball-shaped heavenly bodies that orbit the sun

solar system (SO ler SIS tim) — the sun, planets and other heavenly bodies that revolve around the sun

tide (TIDE) — the changing level of oceans as they react to the moon's gravity

INDEX

axis 9
darkness 16
daylight 16
equator 19
fall 20
gravity 11, 22
heat 14
light 14
Mercury 6
moon 11, 22
northern hemisphere 19
north pole 9, 19
orbit 6, 9, 11
planets 5, 6

seasons 20
solar system 5, 11
southern hemisphere 19
south pole 9, 19
space 5, 11
spring 20
summer 20
sun 5, 6, 14, 16, 20
sunlight 20
tides 22
Venus 6
winter 20